GOD'S CHARACTER-
LET'S MAKE IT PERSONAL

M. LEONNA GIBSON

authorHOUSE®

AuthorHouse™
1663 Liberty Drive
Bloomington, IN 47403
www.authorhouse.com
Phone: 1 (800) 839-8640

Published by AuthorHouse 05/07/2020

ISBN: 978-1-7283-6056-0 (sc)
ISBN: 978-1-7283-6055-3 (e)

Library of Congress Control Number: 2020907894

Print information available on the last page.

CONTENTS

DEDICATION

In memory of my mom, Sheila Gibson, who saw how I was for many years, but who lived long enough to see who I became after my encounters with God's character.

ACKNOWLEDGEMENTS

Many thanks to my daughter Parish for her support and patience with me on this journey of discovering the power of faith in God's character and the inheritance it affords me to leave with her and my grandchildren. A legacy of truth, faith, and integrity. To every family member I have, the families I was born into, foster families, military family and brothers and sisters in and from the Lord – each and every one of you have uniquely touched my life and impacted my growth and understanding of God in ways that are indescribable. I am eternally grateful to each of you. To Debra Garner, who God decided to bring into my life at just the right time, who supports all that I do to build up and empower others and, her great support in the success of this book.

PROLOGUE

Have you ever had a friend or family member that you met for the first time? You heard about them from other family members or friends who only knew what they heard from others, but that was the extent of what you knew. The day comes when you finally meet that family member or friend and you're wondering what it will be like to get to know this person – what they are really like first-hand and not through what you've heard from others. Did you ever find yourself thinking as you were getting to know that person, *"they're nothing like what I heard"* or *"wow, I can't believe how far off the mark they were about them"?* The reason those kinds of questions came to mind, is because no one can know what another person is like without getting to know them personally first-hand. It is then that you discover the nature and the character of that person by the time you invest with them for yourself.

You get to see the consistency or inconsistencies of their responses and reactions in various situations. As you got to know that family member or friend you began to discover whether you could trust them, count on them, or even confide in them. You got to the point where you didn't have to wonder about how they would react or respond, because you now know their character. Having the view or perception of those other family members or friends dictated your initial response - until you got to know them for yourself.

Getting to know them first-hand provided you pure perspective about their true character and gave you an opportunity to respond to them according to the truth that you discovered personally and not what someone else thought or perceived from their initial impression of them. God and man had a pure relationship at one time before sin entered the human race and separated us. Through that separation by sin, the relationship wasn't the only thing that was lost – one of the other things was our original and proper view of who God really is – this was a tremendous loss we incurred as well.

And though our relationship with God can be restored with faith in what God did through Jesus the Christ on the cross, the restoration of our view of God's nature is not automatic. A relationship needs participation from each party. God began by initiating restoration of our relationship with Him. Here is where we can begin to participate and respond to what God is saying in this book.

We were left with an incorrect view and understanding of God's True nature that left us blaming God, denying God, fighting, and questioning God's True character and accepting every lie about His nature as Truth. We've had assumptions about God and expectations of God that were based on our sin-stained view and opinions of Him and not His true character.

As you read through this book you will discover parts of God's nature, what those parts look like, His knowledge of your view of Him, what He wants you to know about Him and more, through the revelation He has given in this book as well as revelation you will receive for yourself as you read it. You may find yourself thinking, *"Hmm...He's nothing like what I heard"*, or *"I can't believe how far off the mark they were about Him"*. Come into an understanding of some first-hand revelation of God's character and discover through this book and most importantly through revelation you receive from God of what He's really like for yourself.

FOREWORD

A few years back, my closest friend gave me a gift for my birthday, and I remember thinking, "How strange." It was strange for ME but surely not strange to her. This friend always gives me practical things to help make my life manageable because she knows that with my assignment as a pastor with a full-time job, a husband, children, and grandchildren, I need all the help I can get! I knew she meant well but, on this birthday, as I opened the small box, I assumed it was jewelry or a sample of my favorite perfume.

When I opened it, I saw a shiny red thing-a-ma-jig that looked something like a stapler. But it had a USB port and instructions. When she saw my confused face my friend blurted, "It's a portable scanner, you can carry it anywhere and all you have to do is upload it to your laptop." Needless to say, this wonderful invention joined the shelf of other good ideas where a digital pressure cooker, portable phone charger, and other "good intention gadgets" sat. I never found out the true value of these things because I never took the time to find out how they worked, and how they could help my all too busy life.

Unfortunately, that's how many of us are when it comes to finding out the true value of our relationship with God. Most of what we hear sounds good, and even makes us feel good while we're in church, but the idea of feeling close to God for many, is just that, an idea. I have come to realize through time spent in prayer and meditation, that the problem the church has is that most believers of Jesus, know ABOUT God through sermons and teachings, but most don't KNOW God. They don't know His nature, how He thinks, His genuine purpose, and His genuine character.

Since most don't truly know Him, most find it hard to feel a closeness and to truly experience personal encounters that the Lord has carved out individually for His children. We were made for God's purpose, for Him to fill us up with Himself and work through us to influence the earth. We were made to represent heaven on earth, to be ambassadors for Christ. How can we represent who we don't truly know? How can we feel closeness to someone we were never taught to personally know or understand? How can we clearly hear God's voice without being certain of His character, since all that God says and does is true to who He really is?

What if God decided to speak to us directly about Himself, His nature and His own analysis of His nature? In a small church sitting on a corner of an industrial area, God did just that. Through one of His messengers, Apostle M. Leonna Gibson, He revealed much about His true character through biblical references and prophetic insights. That was in 2014. Our church read it, heard it, and studied it. I preached it, meditated on it and like my friend told me about that portable scanner, I told them, "this is valuable for your life, don't sleep on it." Some were excited at first and then put it on the "good for you" shelf. But those who have embraced it, have experienced an intimate perspective of God that has changed the way they see Him, the way they worship, the way they pray, and ultimately the way they see themselves.

God tells us that we are His and He is ours. We were never intended to have a long distant, confused, and lukewarm relationship with Him. Our communication with Him was never intended to be tentative because of fear, guilt, or shame. We were never supposed to be children afraid of being open and honest with our Heavenly Father. To know Him, is to understand His character. When you understand His character, you will get a clear and life-altering view of who He is, who you are, and where your faith should truly be - in His character.

Pastor Debra A. Garner
Purpose Destination Ministries
(formerly A Closer Walk Christian Ministries)

INTRODUCTION

To understand the nature of God, it is important to establish a relationship with Him. Many songs have been written about belonging to God, walking with God, and being a child of God. Some people mistakenly believe that by being born, they are automatically in the family of God. Yet the Word makes it clear that the connection to God comes with a decision and an understanding that only through faith in what God did through Jesus Christ can a relationship begin:

> *[10] For with the heart a person believes [in Christ as Savior] resulting in his justification [that is, being made righteous-being freed of the guilt of sin and made acceptable to God]; and with the mouth he acknowledges and confesses [his faith openly], resulting in and confirming [his] salvation. Romans 10:10 Amplified Bible*

> *[12] And there is salvation in no one else; for there is no other name under heaven that has been given among people by which we must be saved [for God has provided the world no alternative for salvation]." Acts 4:12 New Living Translation*

A married couple gets to know the character of one another through day to day experiences as they are committed to sharing a life together. The marriage relationship began with a declaration that ended with two words, "I do" or "I will." Our relationship with God begins with a declaration of faith in God for what He did through the Lord Jesus Christ. Let us begin by making sure that we are truly His and then we can be in a position to get to know Him better and to see Him from the proper perspective - His.

Accepting Christ as Savior

Almighty God, I acknowledge that I am only human, I am limited in every way, and I do not know all that I think I know or thought I knew. I have been living this life like I know what to do with it. But I confess, from the deepest parts of me, that I do not really have a clue. Therefore, I acknowledge my need for a Savior. I acknowledge my need for the One that made me and knows me better than anyone and knew me before anyone else could. I acknowledge that you sent your son Jesus to die on the cross so that man's relationship with you could be restored and that we would not have to die but live forever in relationship with you. Therefore today, I make a decision to accept what you did through your son Jesus Christ in order to restore your relationship with me, and I believe He died and that You raised Him to life so that I can receive your restoration of eternal life and relationship right now. I thank you today for receiving me back as your child because of what Christ did, and not for any good works I could ever do. Today, I receive you as My Father and my God, forever, AMEN.

Getting to Know God—From His Perspective

Father God, Thank you for making yourself available to me and for making provision through the Cross of Christ for me; to know you personally, to talk to you, and you to me, to call on you, to be myself with you - is a wonderful privilege. Thank you in advance for opening my eyes with understanding and revelation of your wonderful nature. I heard it said that you are the Great I Am but grant me personal revelation of that part of You and every other part of your nature that will cause my faith in who You are to soar. Thank you for hearing my heart today, as I seek to know you better. I thank you now for the revelation that will lead to the removal of every hindrance and obstacle in this journey to know you better. Thank you for granting me understanding of who you are and how to fully experience all that you are as I walk with you. Give me to know what it means to truly honor you today and every day. In Jesus name. Amen.

Characteristics of God

While not an exhaustive list, we will look at the following characteristics that speak of the true nature of God:

- Infinite
- Omniscient
- Holy
- Omnipresent
- Omnipotent
- Transcendent
- Righteous

- Sovereign
- Faithful
- Immutable

Oftentimes, people handle things and situations differently when they know or understand the nature of those circumstances or the nature of people. They're usually not as uptight or even annoyed as they would generally be because they know the nature of the people and/or the situation.

Having an incorrect view or understanding of God's nature _will most certainly_ dictate our response and communication to Him and how we see our relationship with Him. A person who sees God as mean and distant, will be quick to blame Him for things that seem to go wrong or do not turn out the way they hope. If it has been difficult to hear God's voice or feel His presence, it is easy to believe or feel you are being ignored or neglected if you do not truly know Him.

These are some of the things that can be revealed to you personally as you gain understanding of the nature of God:

- _Who you are & your purpose_
- _Deliverance/Healing_
- _The enemy's opposition to God's Character_
- _Truth vs. Lies_
- _Peace & Joy_

This book is _not_ designed to give you a formula and/or serve up answers on a platter, but to lead you to the character of the _only_ One who has all the answers to your life's many questions and the personal revelation you need to navigate your way to His purpose. Having a proper understanding of who He is, enables us to ask the appropriate questions about His will for our lives as opposed to expecting, demanding, and requiring Him to deliver on things that align with our will instead of His. How can we expect a lion not to devour an antelope when it's in his nature to do so? Or expect a cat to cuddle up with a buffalo? We would be looking for these animals to behave in a way that is not in accordance with their nature and that would be an unrealistic expectation. And so it is the same with us and God. Because God knows all about us He doesn't have any unrealistic expectations about us. But because we don't really know His nature, we have all kinds of expectations of God based on what we think we know about Him. How can you trust or follow or require of someone you don't really know or someone you've only heard about?

We will now look at revelation that I received directly from God regarding a few of His characteristics. We can discover how knowing His nature can truly minister to us and lead us into natural and personal connection and communication with God through His character. Knowing His nature can lead to knowing who we truly are to Him and why we were made.

CHAPTER 1

INFINITE

Without any limits; endless, vast, immeasurable, and universally omnipresent.

The human mind longs to prove the existence or significance of a thing by how it can be measured. What does the future hold? When is the world coming to an end? How much grief and sorrow can a heart endure? What is the purpose for mankind? These intellectual reasonings can make it difficult to grasp God's infinite nature, because we are used to things having a distinct end and beginning. Our ignorance of His nature compels us to go as far as we can go in our limited way of thinking and to exhaust ourselves into trying to understand from our intellect what can only be revealed by the Living God.

> *And may you be able to feel and understand, as all God's children should, how long, how wide, how deep, and how high his love really is; and to experience this love for yourselves, though it is so great that you will never see the end of it or fully know or understand it. And so at last you will be filled up with God Himself. Ephesians 3:18-19 The Living Bible*

<u>The Lord spoke to me about His infinite nature and said:</u>

This part of My nature is to show you of how immeasurable My love, mercy, patience and kindness is concerning you; it tells you that there is no end to My love for you; that there is no end to My patience and My kindness concerning you; it is that which can't be measured or contained, therefore My plans for you can't be contained or limited by any adversary. It also tells you that the power of Christ's death, burial and resurrection can't be measured; that His perfect Blood and its power has no limits and no end. His blood is perfect, and its purpose and power has been perfectly executed on the Cross to restore you to dominion and power over any trial, any tribulation or trauma you may face.

<u>Inviting the Infinite Nature of God</u>

In the times we devote to spending with God, we can focus on this side of God and allow Him to come into places where we see limitations. We see limits on how well we will do as parents, teachers, supervisors, leaders, etc. We look at how well we will do on our jobs, and we ponder the limits we expect to have when it comes to things like tuition, business endeavors, and retirements and all the things we look forward to in our future. These areas and the limits we see around them flood our minds every day. It is in those places where we see limits, is where we can invite a limitless God. It is His character; it was and is His very nature that has kept me and continues to sustain me when the odds are against me. Faith in His nature, and His endless ability enables me to stand firm when He speaks despite how things look or feel. These are the times and seasons that you discover what's reliable and trustworthy, and what's not. I know that no matter what, God will remain the same and over the years that was (many times) all I had to hold on to. A scripture may not come to mind, but God will say, "I want you to think on who I am, think on this or that part of My nature that I revealed to you". When I'm reminded that there is no beginning or end to a self-existing God, I remember that though troubles always begin, they definitely will end, always with a teachable lesson. I learned how to look for what I needed to see and not for the end of the trouble. The infinite nature of God is above anything I may face now or in the future.

> *[7] "Can you discover the depths of God? Can you [by searching] discover the limits of the Almighty [ascend to His heights, extend to His widths, and comprehend His infinite perfection]? [8] "His wisdom is as high as the heights of heaven. What can you do? It is deeper than Sheol (the nether world, the place of the dead). What can you know? [9] "It is longer in measure [and scope] than the earth, And broader than the sea. Job 11:7-9 Amplified Bible*

CHAPTER 2

OMNISCIENT

All-knowing; having all knowledge of the universe past, present, and future

*Lord, you know everything there is to know about
me. Psalm 139:1 The Passion Translation*

What God knows about us has never hindered his plan
and purpose for our lives. Saul (later known as Paul), spent
years punishing those who followed Christ and God saw and
knew about every murderous threat. He saw every act Saul
was committed to in locking up followers and had first-hand
knowledge of his agreement to allow the public stoning of
Stephen *(Acts 7:58).* Here we see how the conversion of Saul
transformed his view of Jesus and how he became a leader in
the New Testament church. God knew his future, understood
his past, and was merciful in his present. What He knew about
Saul, what He saw him doing, and the plots and schemes
of his heart, did not stop God from appearing to him on a
dusty road called Damascus, changing his life in ways he never
would've expected. This radical change in Saul's life went on
to have a tremendous impact on God's people during that time
and continues to do the same throughout the generations to
this day.

> *⁹ Meanwhile, Saul was uttering threats with every
> breath and was eager to kill the Lord's followers.
> So, he went to the high priest. ² He requested*

letters addressed to the synagogues in Damascus, asking for their cooperation in the arrest of any followers of the Way he found there. He wanted to bring them—both men and women—back to Jerusalem in chains.

³ As he was approaching Damascus on this mission, a light from heaven suddenly shone down around him. ⁴ He fell to the ground and heard a voice saying to him, "Saul! Saul! Why are you persecuting me?" ⁵ "Who are you, lord?" Saul asked. And the voice replied, "I am Jesus, the one you are persecuting! ⁶ Now get up and go into the city, and you will be told what you must do." ⁷ The men with Saul stood speechless, for they heard the sound of someone's voice but saw no one!

⁸ Saul picked himself up off the ground, but when he opened his eyes, he was blind. So, his companions led him by the hand to Damascus. ⁹ He remained there blind for three days and did not eat or drink. ¹⁰ Now there was a believer in Damascus named Ananias. The Lord spoke to him in a vision, calling, "Ananias!" "Yes, Lord!" he replied. ¹¹ The Lord said, "Go over to Straight Street, to the house of Judas. When you get there, ask for a man from Tarsus named Saul. He is praying to me right now. ¹² I have shown him a vision of a man named Ananias coming in and laying hands on him so he can see again."

13 "But Lord," exclaimed Ananias, "I've heard many people talk about the terrible things this man has done to the believers in Jerusalem! 14 And he is authorized by the leading priests to arrest everyone who calls upon your name." 15 But the Lord said, "Go, for Saul is my chosen instrument to take my message to the Gentiles and to kings, as well as to the people of Israel. 16 And I will show him how much he must suffer for my name's sake." 17 So Ananias went and found Saul. He laid his hands on him and said, "Brother Saul, the Lord Jesus, who appeared to you on the road, has sent me so that you might regain your sight and be filled with the Holy Spirit." 18 Instantly something like scales fell from Saul's eyes, and he regained his sight. He got up and was baptized. Acts 9:1-18 New Living Translation

The Lord spoke to me about His Omniscient nature and said:

The depth of My knowledge is boundless; because I am all knowing there is nothing that I don't already know about your past, present, and future. It means that there is nothing that will ever surprise Me or anything that will catch Me off-guard about you or anything you do or face; that I don't have any of the expectations you think I have because I already know what you're going to do in advance.

So, in order for you to disappoint Me you would have to surprise Me. Disappointment implies that there is an expectation, and since I know the entire nature of man, what you will do, each and every moment, past, present or future, YOU CANNOT DISAPPOINT ME. This part of Me speaks to the part of you that is overcome with shame, condemnation, and guilt over what you struggle to move past.

It was My omniscience that knew man would fall, and I put a plan of redemption in place before man fell. This part of My character speaks to the spirit of rejection that plagues you and tells you that nobody cares about you. I made man with a need for safety, belonging, esteem, and fulfillment of purpose. I would never create a need in you and purposely never meet it nor would I have full knowledge of what you need and then reject you when you make me your Source.

Inviting the Omniscient Nature of God

Everything that Saul did was already known by God before it was carried out. This all-knowing part of God's nature was never meant to scare us or have us looking over our shoulder. Having access to this part of who God is can relieve us of the weight and heaviness associated with the standards of perfection that we place on ourselves. Knowing this part of God's nature can deliver us into a place of peace – about the future, about daily provisions, etc. God knows us and had a plan for our lives before we were born. He knows us better than we know ourselves. No matter how carefully we keep secrets from others, we have no secrets from God. I can invite the omniscient nature of God into the daily activities of my life when I see, accept, and embrace that God knows everything about me and that it's a good thing.

I remember when I first discovered God's all-knowing nature. It was amazing yet comforting. This is when I discovered that I could be myself, that it was pointless to try and present myself a certain way to someone who already knew every past, present and future detail about me. I thought to myself, how silly of me! There was a tremendous peace in knowing that I was accepted by Someone who knew what I knew about me and infinitely more. What was familiar throughout my life was rejection and abandonment like many people. So encountering this part of God was mind blowing and beautiful. This part of His nature opened up a whole new way of experiencing and communicating with God. He knows every second, everything I would do or anything I have done in the past and regardless of what He has seen and knows—He still loves me and still has a purpose for me. As long as we feel shame, we won't bring up things we have done or said when we're communicating with God. As long as we avoid sharing certain things or "that" thing with Him, that time will likely feel empty and unfulfilling. It becomes a superficial appointment we keep out of obligation when we're not being honest or when we are afraid He won't pay attention to us because of what He knows.

Yet God says the very part of Him we run from is the part of Him that we can have the most fulfilling encounter with.

It's more than just sharing what's going on, how we feel, or memorizing scriptures. This is the place of experiencing who God is while doing these things. Knowing His nature can change how you share with Him, what you memorize, how you meditate and your confidence before Him. It's okay to ask the Lord to help you see Him as this omniscient God who loves and accepts you, who embraces you while knowing everything about you. He has seen the most shameful things, the worst of the worst, the most embarrassing and unspeakable things about you and still wants to share all that He is with you. Every thought that produces every action, He already knows. You have the privilege to know Him beyond all levels of intellect and reasoning.

> *² You perceive every movement of my heart and soul, and you understand my every thought before it even enters my mind. ³⁻⁴ You are so intimately aware of me, Lord. You read my heart like an open book and you know all the words I'm about to speak before I even start a sentence! You know every step I will take before my journey even begins. Psalm 139:2-4 The Passion Translation*

CHAPTER 3

HOLY

To be set apart; utterly pure, separated from sin; perfect moral purity

Perfection. Without flaws or blemish or fault. Directly or indirectly, that is what mankind longingly tries to achieve and it is the very thing we often mishandle with the nature of God. Unfortunately, when we think about His holiness it often takes us to a place of judgment or incurred wrath of some kind that we anticipate will find us if we do or don't do something. We sing about His holiness, and we participate in various forms of what is perceived or defined as worship. However, we can't worship God without knowing or receiving a revelation of His nature – who He is. So, I'm not truly singing or worshiping His holiness until I get a revelation of it. Truth, integrity, and faithfulness flows out of His holy nature. Our perception is colored by so much of what we're used to seeing that an encounter with His holiness could be easily missed or misinterpreted. This can cause God to seem uninterested, unreal, and out of reach.

Yet God has revealed that nothing about Him is out of our reach. When Moses asked God to confirm His presence by revealing His glory (the dwelling or settling of His divine presence), the Lord complied because He looked favorably on Moses despite the sins of the people of Israel. A reflection of the best of Himself, His brilliant unblemished goodness, shone brightly as Moses watched Him pass by. His goodness speaks to virtue, complete uprightness, the highest moral standard, and purity. This journey on earth is not about us attaining perfection but accessing and interacting with a Perfect God so we can be vessels for His purpose with His influence that reflects integrity and truth in and throughout the earth.

> *12 One day Moses said to the Lord, "You have been telling me, 'Take these people up to the Promised Land.' But you haven't told me whom you will send with me. You have told me, 'I know you by name, and I look favorably on you.' 13 If it is true that you look favorably on me, let me know your ways so I may understand you more fully and continue to enjoy your favor. And remember that this nation is your very own people."*

> *14 The Lord replied, "I will personally go with you, Moses, and I will give you rest—everything will be fine for you." 15 Then Moses said, "If you don't personally go with us, don't make us leave this place. 16 How will anyone know that you look favorably on me—on me and on your people—if you don't go with us? For your presence among us sets your people and me apart from all other people on the earth."*

> *17 The Lord replied to Moses, "I will indeed do what you have asked, for I look favorably on you, and I know you by name." 18 Moses responded, "Then show me your glorious presence." 19 The Lord replied, "I will make all my goodness pass*

before you, and I will call out my name, Yahweh, before you. For I will show mercy to anyone I choose, and I will show compassion to anyone I choose. ²⁰ But you may not look directly at my face, for no one may see me and live."

²¹ The Lord continued, "Look, stand near me on this rock. ²² As my glorious presence passes by, I will hide you in the crevice of the rock and cover you with my hand until I have passed by. ²³ Then I will remove my hand and let you see me from behind. But my face will not be seen."

Exodus 33:12-23 New Living Translation

The Lord spoke to me about His Holy nature and said:

This part of My nature says that there is no way that I would lead you to sin or lead you into an activity that would cause you to sin. There are times in your life where you don't feel Me near and there are times in your life where you're wondering where I am. It is in times like these that your decision to sin moves you away from Me, for I cannot leave you; but the sin that you make excuses to remain in, separates you from Me and My good plans for you.

This part of my character is to show you that my plans for you and my thoughts toward you are pure. I am not out to get you or punish you, for punishment is for My enemies, not My children; I have cleansed you, set you apart for my kingdom purpose, to bring out of you the king I put in you. For I am not demanding perfection from you, but I do want you to see how and why you are set apart from all I created; as you have been made in My likeness, so it has been given to you to govern earth even as I govern heaven.

I am able in My pureness to purge you of the sin that you find to be in your heart. In My holiness, I am able to purge those thoughts that cause you to think impurely, carry out things that are not pure, or thoughts that cause you to talk yourself out of what I decreed for you to be and to do. I am able to purify, and I am able to cleanse you.

This part of My nature is able to set you apart from anything and everything that has tried to keep you away from My original purpose for you. In My Holiness I am able to preserve you, the purpose that I placed in you, and the gifts that I put in you regardless of what has happened in your life, regardless of what's going on even now.

Inviting the Holiness of God

Inviting the Holiness of God into your day to day life is not about wearing a robe, or a cross, or some fancy outfit. It's not about having your bible laid out on your desk throughout the workday or hanging palms and loads of scriptures on your message board. In fact, many a people have been judged and criticized for not doing those very things and more. This judgment and critical treatment have caused many to distance themselves from God feeling like they don't measure up because they don't do those things. That based on status quo, they're not holy enough to go before God.

I've witnessed the influential impact of ministry leaders on many believers who think they are not holy because they're not in a pulpit or they don't know enough scripture. While some of that thinking is from insecurity and lack of confidence, a good bit of it is based on what believers see and don't see modeled before them. We make the mistake of presenting holiness as being based on works and we condemn the very people that God handpicked and set apart for His purpose. God revealing this part of His nature to me was made easier by the revelation of other parts of Him.

My revelation of God's omniscience and other characteristics made it easier to embrace and to handle His holy nature without trying to attain some level of perfection based on works. Though I was this homegirl from Philly, God was not my homeboy or my dog! He was higher than upstairs! He was the Most High God that deserved the deepest and greatest respect I could give. But that as Holy as He revealed Himself to be, He wanted to live in and through me! God's holiness should be revered and honored. But it is important to understand what holiness is and what it's not from God's perspective and allow His Spirit to reveal the practicality of it in our lives. Yes, it means being set apart, but not setting others apart because they're not wearing what we wear or sharing the same title or position we share. God's idea of setting us apart is exclusively for His purposes, not our agendas. Inviting God's holiness into your day to day life is about inviting Him to reveal the areas of my life where I may be lacking integrity, to reveal the places in my life where I may be associating and forming alliances with people void of moral standards in their decision making. Things that I'm not aware of, things that can hinder God's purpose. God can shine His light in any area, not to embarrass you, but to reveal what is necessary so that your heart is pure and your conscious is clear.

So, you're okay to invite His holiness into places and spaces within you that lack His light and His truth. If you've believed and accepted what God did through Jesus Christ on the cross, then you undoubtedly belong to Him, set apart for Him, to be a light for Him in a world darkened with sin.

> [5] *This is the message [of God's promised revelation] which we have heard from Him and now announce to you, that God is Light [He is holy, His message is truthful, He is perfect in righteousness], and in Him there is no darkness at all [no sin, no wickedness, no imperfection]. 1 John 1:5 Amplified Bible*

CHAPTER 4

OMNIPRESENT

Present everywhere at the same time

When we are at our lowest is the very time, we may doubt that God is truly with us. Our emotions and thoughts of despair can be so loud that it may seem like we are on our own in trying to figure out a solution to our trials and circumstances. A God so great wouldn't be interested in who I am or what I have going on. We may dwell on the fact that since we can't see God, that maybe He is not truly real; since He is invisible to us, maybe we are invisible to Him as well. This can magnify feelings of rejection that make it difficult to embrace the thought of a God who can be so far away yet be so very near. He's the maker of heaven and earth, how could I have an expectation that He would visit me or even speak to me? Because out of all that His hands have made, you are the only thing made in His image. That makes you worth paying attention to, that makes you worth speaking to, that makes your life and everything going on it worth getting involved in.

> 23 *"Am I only a God nearby," declares the* Lord, *"and not a God far away?* 24*Who can hide in secret places so that I cannot see them?" declares the* Lord. *"Do not I fill heaven and earth?" declares the* Lord. *Jeremiah 23:23-24 NIV*

Throughout Scripture, the Lord often reassured those who followed Him by reminding them of His presence. When Joshua, Moses' successor, began leading the children of Israel *(Joshua 1:1-9)*, the Lord encouraged Him by saying in many words *"I will be with you."* When Gideon was called to lead Israel *(Judges 6)*, God reassured Him by saying *"I am with you."* As Jesus was leaving the earth after His resurrection *(Matthew 28:19-20)*, He comforted and instructed His disciples by saying, *"I am with you always."*

The Lord spoke to me about His Omnipresent nature and said:

In My omnipresence, you can be assured that there is nothing you need to try to hide from Me. In My omnipresence, I have an intimate look at things in your life that you can only see the surface of, Your attempt to try to hide things from Me, your attempt to create a hiding place through things, people and places, prevents this part of My Nature from ministering to you. It shuts out My desire to show you what things really look like, to show you what it's going to look like, to show you what it really is versus what you think.

This part of My nature shows you that I can be present while ministering to your heart, holding your future, and delivering you from your past. This part of My nature has the ability to minister to every part of you at the same time, in every area of your life; your past hurts, present circumstances while preparing you

for the plans that I have towards you, to give you a future and a hope.

This part of My nature can minister to the abandonment and the loneliness that weighs on you. It can remind you that because I am everywhere at the same time all the time, in the fullness of My being. My loving reminders of who you are can reach you no matter how low or deeply depressed you may feel. No matter how abandoned, lonely and in despair you may feel at times, I will be there. My being everywhere at the same time tells you that you will never need to feel alone. You will never need to feel abandoned or feel so low that My Spirit can't reach you or My Words can't find you and sustain you. No matter where you are, there I AM.

Inviting the Omnipresence of God

When feelings of loneliness and isolation overpower you, it is an opportunity to invite the omnipresent nature of God into that space and place in your life. There are thoughts that can enter your mind for the purpose of deceiving and ultimately leading you into places of doubt and despair. These kinds of thoughts take you back to moments in your life where you felt the loneliest or the most forgotten. These thoughts, with enough meditation, can convince you that God is nowhere to be found, that you may as well end it, or what's the use, nobody else cares, so why should I. This can happen with believers, particularly when past traumas and tragedies still have a hold on you. I've known so many times throughout my life feeling completely alone. When I first accepted Christ as savior of my life, I was extremely broken and I didn't know what it meant to not feel all alone. Being raised in foster homes from the time I was born and moving from one place to another even after those years, there was still no real sense of belonging anywhere or to anyone. Constantly being walked away from or abandoned left what seemed like a permanent stain in my way of thinking and convinced me for years that no matter how many people were around, I was still all alone. Those feelings drove me to a life of living in a bottle. I felt that drinking as much alcohol as I could find was the only thing that could keep me from having to face the loneliness and the rejection. I thought if I could drink myself into a comatose state, perhaps death would meet me half-way. Living that way and then becoming His and encountering this part of God's nature was completely surreal. I discovered that not only was I not all alone, but that I would never again have to feel alone because this part of Him brought an assurance of His unchangeable nature.

When you know the truth, that there is never a time when God is not with us, never a time when He drops the ball and forgets about us, never a time when He deserts us, His omnipresence can give us the hope we need in those moments when no one else is around. It is in these times when we can be reminded of this part of His nature. Invite this part of God into those times of aloneness and abandonment, or times when you find yourself softly asking questions like "Why am I really here?" "Does anybody really care about me?". Allow Him to remind you of who you are to Him, refer to that revelation He gave you the day or week before, and remember the assurance He made to many in the Bible including Moses, Joshua, Gideon and all of the disciples who followed Jesus who would carry the good news of the Kingdom: *"I am with you and I will never leave you."*

> [15] *For the high and exalted One He who inhabits eternity, Whose name is Holy says this, "I dwell on the high and holy place, But also with the contrite and humble in spirit In order to revive the spirit of the humble And to revive the heart of the contrite [overcome with sorrow for sin]. Isaiah 57:15 Amplified Bible*

CHAPTER 5

OMNIPOTENT

All powerful; Unlimited, inexhaustible
power; Almighty, ruler of all

God's omnipotence is a greatly misunderstood aspect of His character. When we hear that the Lord has the power to do all things and can never, ever fail, we may wonder why cancer persists, babies die, families break up, wars continue, and hunger never ceases in many pockets of the world. God is powerful, but His power works through people He chooses on earth for His specific purposes. It was the power of God that caused a barren woman to give birth to a prophet who would prepare the way for the coming of Jesus and it was the power of God that conceived Jesus so that He could come into the earth to restore God's original order and re-position mankind to manage the earth according to His original intent

The omnipotence of God is demonstrated all throughout the Bible, but many of us don't know His power in our own lives personally. One of the things to remember about God is that He does NOT bully or barge His way into our lives. Every part of God's nature is that of the Truest Gentleman. As much as He adores mankind, He will not impose who He is on us. It is up to us to welcome Him and every part of who He is into the areas of our heart. Power for miracles and signs are not the only displays of God's omnipotence. This great power is meant to manifest through His Spirit in how we live out our purpose and how we influence and impact the generations that follow.

> ²⁶ *In the sixth month of Elizabeth's pregnancy, God sent the angel Gabriel to Nazareth, a village in Galilee,* ²⁷ *to a virgin named Mary. She was engaged to be married to a man named Joseph, a descendant of King David.* ²⁸ *Gabriel appeared to her and said, "Greetings, favored woman! The Lord is with you!"* ²⁹ *Confused and disturbed, Mary tried to think what the angel could mean.* ³⁰ *"Don't be afraid, Mary," the angel told her, "for you have found favor with God!*

> ³¹ *You will conceive and give birth to a son, and you will name him Jesus.* ³² *He will be very great and will be called the Son of the Most High. The Lord God will give him the throne of his ancestor David.* ³³ *And he will reign over Israel forever; his Kingdom will never end!"* ³⁴ *Mary asked the angel, "But how can this happen? I am a virgin."* ³⁵ *The angel replied, "The Holy Spirit will come upon you, and the power of the Most High will overshadow you. So the baby to be born will be holy, and he will be called the Son of God.*

> ³⁶ *What's more, your relative Elizabeth has become pregnant in her old age! People used to say she was barren, but she has conceived a son and is now in her sixth month.* ³⁷ *For the word of God will never fail."*

38 Mary responded, "I am the Lord's servant. May everything you have said about me come true." And then the angel left her.

Luke 1:26-38 New Living Translation

5 When Herod was king of Judea, there was a Jewish priest named Zechariah. He was a member of the priestly order of Abijah, and his wife, Elizabeth, was also from the priestly line of Aaron. 6 Zechariah and Elizabeth were righteous in God's eyes, careful to obey all of the Lord's commandments and regulations. 7 They had no children because Elizabeth was unable to conceive, and they were both very old.

8 One day Zechariah was serving God in the Temple, for his order was on duty that week. 9 As was the custom of the priests, he was chosen by lot to enter the sanctuary of the Lord and burn incense. 10 While the incense was being burned, a great crowd stood outside, praying. 11 While Zechariah was in the sanctuary, an angel of the Lord appeared to him, standing to the right of the incense altar. 12 Zechariah was shaken and overwhelmed with fear when he saw him.

13 But the angel said, "Don't be afraid, Zechariah! God has heard your prayer. Your wife, Elizabeth, will give you a son, and you are to name him John. 14 You will have great joy and gladness, and many will rejoice at his birth, ¹⁵ for he will be great in the eyes of the Lord. He must never touch wine or other alcoholic drinks. He will be filled with the Holy Spirit, even before his birth. ¹⁶ And he will turn many Israelites to the Lord their God.

¹⁷ He will be a man with the spirit and power of Elijah. He will prepare the people for the coming of the Lord. He will turn the hearts of the fathers to their children, and he will cause those who are rebellious to accept the wisdom of the godly." ¹⁸ Zechariah said to the angel, "How can I be sure this will happen? I'm an old man now, and my wife is also well along in years."

¹⁹ Then the angel said, "I am Gabriel! I stand in the very presence of God. It was He who sent me to bring you this good news! ²⁰ But now, since you didn't believe what I said, you will be silent and unable to speak until the child is born. For my words will certainly be fulfilled at the proper time." Luke 1:5-20 New Living Translation

The Lord spoke to me about His Omnipotence and said:

This part of My nature speaks to you regarding the many struggles in your heart and mind, the defeat, the inferiority, the inadequacy and yes even the worthlessness; all the situations that have brought you to a place where you feel overtaken by what's happening or when you feel like you are not going to rise above where and who you've been for such a long time. You've had relationships that have caused you to see yourself as less than who you truly are.

The war zone in your mind tells you that you are what they said you are, you will never be this or that because of where you've been or who your parents are or because of who you've been with. This part of My nature wants you to see and know that there is no struggle, trauma, level of inadequacy, depth of defeat, or place of worthlessness that has the power to overtake you, when My Unlimited power is at work in you.

There is no struggle in your mind that you will encounter that will undermine My Unlimited power at work in you; Power belongs to Me. There is no war zone bad enough, no struggle great enough, no pain strong enough to withstand My Unlimited power at work in and through your life. I have restored to you what was lost in Eden; therefore, you have My power through My Spirit, who lives in you, to withstand any and every adversary that would try to overpower you. My power at work in you cannot be restrained or stopped by anything or anyone in creation. My power is greater than your pain, My strength is stronger than your struggle; there is nothing that has been created or manufactured, nothing that anyone has ever done or could ever do that is greater than My unlimited power at work in you.

<u>Inviting the Omnipotence of God</u>

We have often heard that God is powerful and can do anything, but we aren't often taught that His power on earth is manifested through us. Invite the omnipotence of God by agreeing with what His Word says about you, by coming in agreement with what He reveals to you. God is mighty, strong, and powerful but much of His power is shown on the earth by what He is permitted to do through us. When we welcome this part of God's nature into our hearts and in the different areas of our life, we are acknowledging this part of His nature to be supreme over any other resource and any other means of capability we may have at our disposal. We're inviting the superiority of His strength, wisdom, and insight to accomplish through us the smallest to the greatest tasks. We are giving God permission to enter every space and place in our hearts so He can build, encourage, and develop our confidence in areas where we expect to fail or fall. It's important that we invite God when we need His words in our mouths to build others, to respond to opportunities that will inspire and influence the hopeless and the oppressed to a place of liberty and to provoke and enlighten those of us that think church attendance is enough.

Encountering this part of God's nature so many years ago enabled me to embrace the possibility that years of deep-seated hatred could no longer be in my heart; that I could walk in the real love of God toward the very people I had stored hatred for. I despised my mother and father for many years. It wasn't until Christ saved my whole life, and began to reveal Himself to me, that I moved from frustration and fury to forgiveness. I needed a revelation of a power that far exceeded my thoughts and emotions. I needed to see that what looked and felt impossible wasn't impossible after all. I needed to see that His unlimited power had the ability to turn my heart of stone into a pillow of compassion. Getting a revelation of this part of God's nature brought me hope and healing in a place within me that had become cold, calloused, and bitter. So, it's okay to invite this part of who God is by admitting and acknowledging you are powerless without Him and helpless without His help. It really is okay to admit these things to God. One of the greatest revelations we need as believers is that He is our Source. That must be a revelation and not just another message or a soundbite that sounds good or profound. His purpose for us can't be accomplished without Him.

Apostle Paul understood what it meant to experience God's unlimited power when he was shipwrecked three times, beaten with rods, stoned, bitten by a viper and other things he experienced on his journey. He had faith in God's unlimited power in His life and welcomed God into all that he experienced on his journeys into various cities and countries. He knew God personally and had faith in God's nature and not in what He thought or assumed God should do and that faith and confidence was manifested in and after many trials. This can only be done with our participation and submission to what the Lord reveals to us about our levels of trust in our abilities over His, and our need to obtain power on our own.

[10] *"So I'm not defeated by my weakness, but delighted! For when I feel my weakness and endure mistreatment — when I'm surrounded with troubles on every side and face persecution because of my love for Christ — I am made yet stronger. For my weakness becomes a portal to God's power." 2 Corinthians 12:10 The Passion Translation*

CHAPTER 6

TRANSCENDENT

Existing above and independent from; to rise above, surpass, succeed.

To transcend means to exist above and independent from anything else. The Lord God Almighty is the only transcendent being. He created things on earth, beneath the earth, and in the heaven above. Yet He exists above and independent from all of them. All things are upheld by His mighty power. No evil or injustice in the world can change who He is. He is not moved by it, because He exists apart from it. We are shaken by the storms and calamities of life, but God is not. In the book of Job, here is a rich man who had lost his children, his home, his health, and his wealth. God understood Job's agony and recognized his confusion and ignorance about His transcendent nature during his season of great trials. And Job welcomed this part of God's nature and got a great deal of revelation from God. That revelation changed how He saw God and himself.

God Challenges Job's Response to His Transcendence

Then the Lord answered Job from the whirlwind: ²"Who is this that questions my wisdom with such ignorant words?³ Brace yourself like a man, because I have some questions for you, and you must answer them. ⁴ "Where were you when I laid the foundations of the earth? Tell me, if you know so much. ⁵ Who determined its dimensions and stretched out the surveying line?

⁶ What supports its foundations, and who laid its cornerstone ⁷ as the morning stars sang together and all the angels shouted for joy? ⁸ "Who kept the sea inside its boundaries as it burst from the womb, ⁹ and as I clothed it with clouds and wrapped it in thick darkness? ¹⁰ For I locked it behind barred gates, limiting its shores. ¹¹₋I said, 'This far and no farther will you come. Here your proud waves must stop!' ¹² "Have you ever commanded the morning to appear and caused the dawn to rise in the east? ¹³ Have you made daylight spread to the ends of the earth, to bring an end to the night's wickedness? ¹⁴ As the light approaches, the earth takes shape like clay pressed beneath a seal; it is robed in brilliant colors.

¹⁵ The light disturbs the wicked and stops the arm that is raised in violence. ¹⁶ "Have you explored the springs from which the seas come? Have you explored their depths? ¹⁷ Do you know where the gates of death are located? Have you seen the gates of utter gloom? ¹⁸ Do you realize the extent of the earth? Tell me about it if you know! ¹⁹ "Where does light come from, and where does darkness go? ²⁰ Can you take each to its home? Do you know how to get there?

Job 38:1-20 New Living Translation

Job's Perspective Changes and Restoration Follows

Then Job replied to the Lord: ² "I know that you can do anything, and no one can stop you. ³ You asked, 'Who is this that questions my wisdom_ with such ignorance?' It is I—and I was talking about things I knew nothing about, things far too wonderful for me.

⁴ You said, 'Listen and I will speak! I have some questions for you, and you must answer them.' ⁵ I had only heard about you before, but now I have seen you with my own eyes. ⁶ I take back everything I said, and I sit in dust and ashes to show my repentance."

Job 42:1-6 New Living Translation

The Lord spoke to me about His Transcendence and said:

This part of My nature can minister to that part of you that feels insignificant; that part of you that feels like you're not important, that part of you that disqualifies yourself, or that makes you beat yourself up because you make so many mistakes, or you don't get it right all or most of the time. You've been made to feel like you don't matter, you were walked away from as if you weren't important, or you were made to feel like what you had to say or what you wanted to contribute didn't have any value.

Yet it is My transcendent nature that comes to tell you that I who exists far and above all I have created, apart from anything that has been made, I who transcends all that exists, I who do not need that which I made in order to exist, chose to make man in my image and give them a territory called earth to rule and subdue – to be sovereign in the earth even as I am the Sovereign over the heavens, I chose to redeem you to the place of dominion that is yours, that My kingdom would permeate the earth.

I made this choice because I made you for My pleasure, in My image and to be a reflection of Me and My Kingdom in the earth.

I didn't <u>need</u> to have a relationship with you, I made a <u>choice</u> to have a relationship with you and to restore your position as My child. I made a choice, regardless of the fall of mankind, to redeem you to the place of dominion that is yours, that My kingdom would come, and My will would be done on the earth as it is in heaven.

There was nothing insignificant, unimportant, or without value about you when I made you. There is no way that you can disqualify what I qualified beforehand. From where I'm sitting, I am able to see every mistake, and everywhere you have messed up.

I am able to see everywhere that you have missed it. Just as I transcend, so does My kingdom purpose concerning you, for My ways are far beyond anything you can imagine.

My love for you transcends and exists high above where you messed up, my forgiveness transcends and exists high above where you missed it. That's why you will never miss it so much that I would forsake you, dismiss you, or punish you; for I already know that you will miss it. I already know that you will mess up, and it is in this part of My nature that you will discover that I made a choice to redeem you, even though I am Self-Existent and Self-Sufficient, even though I am well able to exist outside of and apart from anything that I have created. It was indeed <u>My choice.</u> I loved you and I chose you with a full knowledge beforehand of anything that you would ever do or anything that you have ever done.

<u>Inviting the Transcendent Nature of God:</u>

In times when we are shaken by great disappointment and self-doubt, we can invite the transcendent nature of God into our heart and into the troubled areas of our life. We have an opportunity to experience God in a very unique way. It may seem like everything is out of control and you are helpless to stop it. When God begins to reveal Himself to us, we are able to see Him above and beyond our struggles. With this part of His nature He reassures us on the inside that His self-existence does not make Him non-existent to us. A revelation of this part of God's nature gives us the ability to recognize that His limitless transcendence does not box Him in from helping us or box us out of getting to know Him personally.

I have known shattered places, so I've met this part of him - and it helped me to know other parts of Him as well. I've had many times and seasons where I was made to feel insignificant and worthless, that because I was a woman, I couldn't minister the Word or because I didn't go to Bible College I don't make the cut. Because I didn't look the part, I didn't belong, because I didn't quote as much scripture or dance when I heard a certain cord from the organ.

I didn't meet the Lord in a service or in Bible College or at a revival at the church down the road. I met Him at work – or should I say, He met me at work where there was no organ, there was no preacher. There was a young girl with a weight of death on her shoulders contemplating suicide and a book given to me that had one recurring verse in it. That day I encountered a glimpse and a revelation of the transcendent nature of God finding me at my core and bringing a truth that saved my life in every way a life could be saved. I began a journey that day that brought me to an understanding of my true value to God. I later discovered that my faith had to be in who He is and not in what He does, for my faith to truly stand. I've learned that there is no growth or maturity that I could reach without knowing, understanding, and engaging the true nature of God. There is personal revelation from God that is at your disposal when you take the time to engage Who God really is according to His nature – that revelation is exclusively for you from Him.

> *8 This plan of mine is not what you would work out, neither are my thoughts the same as yours! 9 For just as the heavens are higher than the earth, so are my ways higher than yours, and my thoughts than yours. Isaiah 55:8-9 The Living Bible*

He exists above and independent of all that He created, yet He made an active choice to create man in His own image, give him an earth to rule and subdue the way He does heaven. It was not God's plan and certainly not God's fault that mankind lost that privilege and allowed sin to enter the human race. But it was God's idea to restore to man what was lost and to send a Perfect Man into the earth to offer a means to that restoration. Man's interaction and relationship with God MUST be voluntary. God does not strong-arm His way into the affairs of our life just because there is a need. He doesn't force His will on us, and He doesn't override our will to do what we choose. A God so far off can only be as near as we allow or permit. He's not a cosmic bellhop waiting on us to give Him a list of everything we want or everything we think He should give us. He doesn't owe us _anything_. And with this part of His nature, we have proof that He doesn't need us to exist.

That is why engaging this part of His nature is a thing of beauty. This is where you discover how significant and valuable you are when you get a personal revelation of this active choice He made, not just to create mankind, but to restore mankind back to relationship with Him by sending Jesus the Christ to the cross to deal with the sin that separated us in the beginning.

By believing and accepting what Jesus selflessly did for us, we don't ever have to be in the dark about who He really is again. The privilege of being His child and the position of ruling and subduing the earth has been restored when we believe and accept what God did through Christ. You can invite this exclusive part of God into the times in your life when you feel like nothing is working. Yes, God sits high, and looks low, but He engages His children when they engage Him and recognize that this relationship was a choice by Him, not a debt He owed. Since He is independent of everything and everyone else, His view of us is independent and exclusive of whatever lies, bad experiences or self-condemnation that comes, to try to convince us that what happens to us is who we are. God is telling us that even though He is exclusive and self-existent, He desires to be involved in day to day activities with us and allow us the opportunity to experience Him the way He truly is.

> [22] *It is He who sits above the circle of the earth, And its inhabitants are like grasshoppers; [It is He] who stretches out the heavens like a veil And spreads them out like a tent to dwell in.*
>
> *Isaiah 40:22 Amplified Bible*

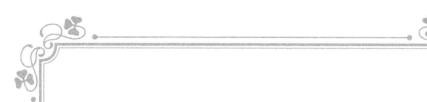

CHAPTER 7

RIGHTEOUS

Morally right and just; uprightness; fair

The righteous nature of God is likely the part of God that we have the biggest issue with. We have an idea of what we believe is right and just in our limited human understanding. Our perception is tainted by culture, opinions and most often, difficult experiences. Yet, God has a global picture of what is fair based on what He sees and what He knows. When we learn to trust this aspect of His nature, we will understand our unrealistic expectations of God concerning what He should or shouldn't do about the injustices of the world and the unfair ways others have treated us. It must be understood that He will only move according to who He is, not who we think He should be based on our limited understanding.

God cannot deny or defy His character under any circumstances - not even out of His love and concern for mankind. Here we see how Jesus responds to a demand for justice from those who caught a woman engaged in adultery. As far as the people were concerned, she broke the law and should be stoned for it. There was no debate on the table. The people of this time are not much different than we are – they only saw one side of a much bigger picture. When we are hurt or mishandled, we demand justice and there is no debate on the table. Jesus didn't see things the way everyone else saw it. He's the only one that saw the bigger picture – she needed a chance at redemption. From God's view, no one is unredeemable – _no one_. Without this big picture view where would you and I be right now?

> [1] _Jesus returned to the Mount of Olives,_ [2] _but early the next morning he was back again at the Temple. A crowd soon gathered, and he sat down and taught them._ [3] _As he was speaking, the teachers of religious law and the Pharisees brought a woman who had been caught in the act of adultery. They put her in front of the crowd._ [4] _"Teacher," they said to Jesus, "this woman was caught in the act of adultery._ [5] _The law of Moses says to stone her. What do you say?"_

> [6] _They were trying to trap him into saying something they could use against him, but Jesus stooped down and wrote in the dust with his_ _finger._ [7] _They kept demanding an answer, so he stood up again and said, "All right, but let the one who has never sinned throw the first stone!"_ [8] _Then he stooped down again and wrote in the dust._

> [9] _When the accusers heard this, they slipped away one by one, beginning with the oldest, until only Jesus was left in the middle of the crowd with the woman._ [10] _Then Jesus stood up again and said to the woman, "Where are your accusers? Didn't even one of them condemn you?"_ [11] _"No, Lord,"_

she said. And Jesus said, "Neither do I. Go and sin no more." John 8:1-11 New Living Translation

As you can see in this passage, Jesus did not respond the way the woman's accusers demanded him to. They wanted Him to condemn her, but instead, He lovingly corrected her and then forgave her. Forgiveness is tied to justice - it's a rights issue. It is important that we are open to receive a revelation of a need to give up our right to our idea of justice. It's seeing our need to trust in God's Righteous nature and the fairness and justice that flows out of that part of Him. That must be revealed to us personally.

The Lord spoke to me about His Righteous nature and said:

This part of My nature speaks to the parts of you that feel like I am ignoring you, ignoring how you feel, ignoring what you've gone through, and ignoring everything that's happening in your life right now. There are parts of you that sometimes feel like I don't love you because of how things have turned out, because things don't feel fair. It doesn't seem like things happened in your favor, or it doesn't seem like things are going to ever happen in your favor. You feel insignificant, like what you go through and how you feel doesn't matter. Most of the time what's happening is that you have a limited view of what's really going on. There's so much that you don't see and because you don't see it, you don't understand the 'why' and the 'what', so you feel like you're being treated unfairly. I have a full view of

everything that's going on; all the people, places and things that are involved, everything that could, would, and/or should happen, I have a full view.

I have all the details to factor in all that's done or not done by anyone, anywhere, at any time. You will NEVER have all the details that I have. I will ALWAYS have ALL the details; therefore, you will never be able to declare that I am unfair without it being a lie. My Perfect nature requires and demands my justice and fairness. I would cease to be perfect if I were unfair.

I will ALWAYS see what you don't see; from everyone's beginning to everyone's end. All are in front of me right now.

I work with what's hidden from some and seen by a few and I work with all that's lying open for all to see; but, there are parts of situations and circumstances that no one else can see but Me. There are parts of different things that happen in your life, different things that occur concerning you that nobody else can see but Me and sometimes, I allow some things instead of other things to occur.

This part of My nature declares My fairness. It declares that I am Just in every decision that I make according to My Word because I have all the facts, all of the truth, and all of the evidence. There is nothing that I don't know about before I allow or cause something to take place about anything going on.

Most things only seem unfair because of your limited view, most things seem unjust because you're not seeing all of what I see. This causes you at times to become angry with Me and to feel as though I am not being fair to you, but if you will allow me to share this part of Myself with you, then you will understand that there are some things that I will allow because I am able to cause all things to work together for your good. I am able to cause all things to work for you and not against you, even though it may look like it's going against you.

It is this part of My nature that has protected you when you were somewhere that you should not have been; when you were hanging out with people that I told you to separate from; when you were making decisions that did not have anything to do with My will and My purpose for you; and when you were choosing to go in one direction when I told you to go in another.

It is My Righteous nature that considers you, that considers My thoughts and plans toward you and the inheritance you have received through the finished work of Christ. It was this part of My nature that remembered My covenant that I made with you.

Inviting the Righteous nature of God

"Lord, people keep hurtin' me, disappointing me and mishandling me and it doesn't look like you're doing anything about it, it's like you don't even care! I thought you were goin'

have my back! I just feel like life is unfair, that Lord, you ain't fair! Why are you taking so long to get them for what they did to me?! How can you love me and let them get way with this! This ain't cool Lord!"

Sound familiar? I had struggled for years to see the fairness in a God who would allow me to be abandoned and rejected repeatedly. And even when I thought I wasn't struggling anymore; I still was because I hadn't encountered the Truth about this part of God's nature. In not being healed from those experiences, I tried to manipulate God's nature to conform to granting me what I felt I should have, do, etc. I wanted the Lord to sway in the direction that would accommodate how I felt. My ever-changing emotions were fighting against a never-changing character of God. I tried to go up against the Lord's solid nature with fluid emotions. The more I denied and dismissed as True the Righteous nature of God and resolved to believe the lies that my circumstances told me about His Righteousness, the more I empowered the sense of injustice I felt.

My emotions put God's Righteous nature on trial and declared this part of His nature to be a big lie. This kept me constantly lashing out at God and not realizing that's what I was doing. My emotions and my thoughts were convinced through situations and experiences, of who God was, creating a perception that caused me to declare Him unfit to be God and unfit to be my Father. Sounds a little wild huh? God revealed this to me, these were real charges I brought against Him. His revelation will reveal what we need to see about Him and ourselves.

This revelation about me and His Righteous nature, was one of the best things that could ever happen to me. It brought tremendous peace to my soul to see this part of God's nature based on what was true and not on what I was determined to think or feel. I didn't know and couldn't see that the choices other people made were not His choices and I couldn't see beyond what I was feeling so deeply during those years of my life. When I encountered the Righteousness of God, I recognized that His view of people and life is bigger than any lens I was seeing through, and that His judgment is always fair and always right, whether I see or know how He responds to situations or not.

God says, "vengeance is mine" but that vengeance will most likely not look anything like what we want, expect or think. It doesn't mean He hasn't exacted vengeance as He said He would. His vengeance is based on ALL the facts and evidence, ours is based on limited information composed of mostly assumptions. Therefore, He is absolutely just in all He does and all He allows.

When we invite the righteous nature of God, we are acknowledging our need to see His view of justice and fairness over our own. It's a trust in God's justice that comes from a revelation of His righteous nature. We recognize that His righteousness is not out to get us or condone others to mishandle us and cause us pain. That perspective goes against every part of His nature that God is revealing to us in this book and further wants to reveal to you. He is not a cruel and unfair God, and once I experienced His moral and gentle nature, I realized my emotions clouded my view and made it difficult for me to see Him as He truly is.

God is not controlling man like he's a robot and pressing a button or switch to move men to do what they do to others. He is also not forcing people to amend for their actions either. I needed a perspective that would allow me to see me, others, and God properly. Who was I to judge God when I didn't have the absolute truth? All the facts and all the evidence were needed to judge those situations and people the way I did – but I didn't even scratch the surface of what I thought I knew was true. A root of bitterness can grow out of ignorance of this part of God's nature. It was like looking in a dirty mirror with smears and spots all over it.

I had to grab hold of the righteous nature of God so I wouldn't harbor bitterness from wrongs done to me anymore. And then—I invited the righteous God to show me His Truth, the real deal. I recognized that with an unlimited view like His, and a limited view like mine, I better stick with His revelation on the affairs of my life. Getting to know this part of His character changed everything for me.

> [1] Out of the stump of David's family will grow a shoot – yes, a new branch bearing fruit from the old root.[2] And the spirit of the lord will rest on him – the Spirit of wisdom and understanding, the Spirit of counsel and might, the Spirit of knowledge and the fear of the Lord. [3] He will delight in obeying the Lord. He will not judge by appearance nor make a decision based on hearsay. [4] He will give

justice to the poor and make fair decisions for the exploited. The earth will shake at the force of his word, and one breath from his mouth will destroy the wicked. ⁵He will wear righteousness like a belt and truth like an undergarment. Isaiah 11:1-5 New Living Translation

CHAPTER 8

SOVEREIGN

Principal (highest in rank), chief, supreme. It speaks first of position, then of power; being above all others in character, importance, excellence; potentate (possessor of great power); Having supreme power or authority

The sovereign nature of God is another aspect of His character that is often mishandled. We struggle with what He controls versus what He has given us His power to control. Yet nothing happens outside of the knowledge of God. All things are either allowed by Him or caused by Him for His purposes and through His perfect will and timing. God's servant Job was committed to God, and Satan needed His permission to test Job with traumatic events in His life. In fact, the tragedies Job endured was an opportunity for him to see how his faith in who God is would stand up against the fiery trials he was about to face.

Faith in who God is doesn't make you exempt from trials and tragedies and it doesn't stop you from having very human responses like tears or sadness. But you're instead reminded of His character and how faithful He is to stay true to that. This becomes the anchor that holds you and keeps you stable in turbulent times. This faith says even if you don't rescue me, I know you can't leave me because your perfect nature won't let you. This faith says I know you didn't cause this, but I'm certain that you can use it and make it work for my good. It was a most painful journey for Job, but the things that occurred in Job's life allowed him to encounter God in a way he never had before. He had every reason to blame God based on a limited knowledge of God, on the events that were taking place back to back. It seemed like he didn't have a chance to respond to one event before another one came right behind it; events that were, to us, unimaginable and horrific. God permitted the enemy to afflict Job because He knew Job better than he knew himself. He knew what Job's response would be during this terrible season in his life – and yet He gave the enemy permission to wreak havoc in every area. Would God allow and permit what I couldn't overcome through Him and cause His purpose concerning me to not be fulfilled? Not at all.

> *7 "Where have you come from?" the Lord asked Satan. Satan answered the Lord, "I have been patrolling the earth, watching everything that's going on." 8 Then the Lord asked Satan, "Have you noticed my servant Job? He is the finest man in all the earth. He is blameless—a man of complete integrity. He fears God and stays away from evil."*

> *9 Satan replied to the Lord, "Yes, but Job has good reason to fear God.*

> *10You have always put a wall of protection around him and his home and his property. You have made him prosper in everything he does. Look how rich he is! 11But reach out and take away everything he has, and he will surely curse you to your face!" 12"All right, you may test him," the Lord said to Satan. "Do whatever you want with everything*

he possesses, but don't harm him physically." So, Satan left the Lord's presence. ¹³One day when Job's sons and daughters were feasting at the oldest brother's house, ¹⁴ a messenger arrived at Job's home with this news: "Your oxen were plowing, with the donkeys feeding beside them, ¹⁵ when the Sabeans raided us. They stole all the animals and killed all the farmhands. I am the only one who escaped to tell you." ¹⁶ While he was still speaking, another messenger arrived with this news: "The fire of God has fallen from heaven and burned up your sheep and all the shepherds. I am the only one who escaped to tell you."

¹⁷ While he was still speaking, a third messenger arrived with this news: "Three bands of Chaldean raiders have stolen your camels and killed your servants. I am the only one who escaped to tell you." ¹⁸ While he was still speaking, another messenger arrived with this news: "Your sons and daughters were feasting in their oldest brother's home. ¹⁹ Suddenly, a powerful wind swept in from the wilderness and hit the house on all sides. The house collapsed, and all your children are dead. I am the only one who escaped to tell you."

²⁰Job stood up and tore his robe in grief. Then he shaved his head and fell to the ground to worship. ²¹ He said, "I came naked from my mother's womb, and I will be naked when I leave. The

Lord gave me what I had, and the Lord has taken it away. Praise the name of the Lord!" [22] *In all of this, Job did not sin by blaming God. Job 1:7-22 New Living Translation*

The Lord spoke to me about His Sovereign nature and said:

This part of My nature is what many of My children struggle with the most. It's one of the parts of My nature that is the most misunderstood and the most misinterpreted. You have been led and many times deceived into believing that because I'm known to be Sovereign, because I am the Supreme Ruler of heaven and earth, that anything displeasing or painful that did happen or is happening in your life, was supposed to automatically or naturally be stopped by Me.

It is hard to understand what you know so little or nothing about My child. It has caused you to be angry with Me to the point that you have stopped praying, sharing, and studying. It has caused you to spend more time questioning "why" I did this or "why" I let this or that happen; until finally your accuser, the devil, "suggests" to you that it's all My fault as to why you're still where you are, or why things didn't go the way you wanted it, or why you don't have this or that yet or why those things are still happening.

My child, there is no part of My character that can be understood with a natural eye or ear.

You have blamed Me for many things that have gone wrong in your life and in the world around you; painful wounds you have received, traumatic experiences that have left you heartbroken. What you don't understand My child, is that the fallen world you live in is not the world that originated with Me, but with sin. I cannot intervene in the affairs of man without man's permission. I am Sovereign over the Heavens, but you My child are the sovereign I made to be on the earth — that is what I meant when I said You were to rule, to have dominion.

My nature will not allow me to violate My own laws. Earth is your jurisdiction. The cross of Christ restored to you the power and ability to restore and heal the earth that's been given back to you. It is sin that caused the fall from dominion and in a sin-filled world, there is pain that did not come from Me. There is heartbreak that did not come from me. There is oftentimes suffering at the hands of another, but I cannot take away man's free will without making him a robot unable to choose. I would then be forcing you to be kind or to love others - but my love does not force. It is not in my nature to bully or to bulldoze, but to extend my Love and My kingdom through you by your choice to be restored to proper relationship with Me.

Inviting the Sovereign Nature of God

The enemy's position was and still is, that if we have the "stuff" we want or need from God, we're "blessed", and all is well. Unfortunately, in many instances he is right, because our skewed view of God causes us to deal with Him like a cosmic cop and a genie. When times of trouble come, we're dialing 911 and other times we're attempting to obey all the "rules" so we can get what we wish for. We can't invite or welcome what we don't understand and expect to get optimum results.

Job knew enough not to curse God, but he also knew enough not to blame God for what was happening in His life. He knew that God wasn't out to get him, that God was not punishing him. A revelation of this part of God's nature will go a long way to discovering how much you don't know about His sovereignty and what's necessary to see to adequately respond to this part of Him. If you'll notice, Job did not respond to his circumstances the way his wife or friends expected or thought he should. They all had their list of reasons why or how he should respond to the horrible events that occurred. He was a father in pain over losing his children, he was a man with property and servants that was reduced to nothing, and that hurt. But his first response was grief – real human grief over his many losses. His understanding of God's sovereignty and I'm sure, other parts of His nature, produced worship. Job fell to the ground and worshipped the Living God after getting the worst news a human being could get. He didn't have a choir nearby or a preacher or worship leader. A revelation he previously received became ever present in his time of trial.

You can only truly worship God when you've gotten a revelation of who He really is. Job's response to tragedy was based on revelations of God's nature. Recognizing who God is and what He's able to do with man's permission and submission is an ongoing challenge when we have been taught for so long that "God can do anything."

When we talk about sovereignty we are talking about a position of rule and authority. God is the ultimate and absolute Sovereign over heaven and earth, but He has given earth to us to manage from a sovereign position, from a place of rulership as those made in His image. God can do anything, but His nature controls and governs what He does. God could decide to take away man's free will and force him to do everything He desires. God could swoop down and force His way into the heart of a person so they can receive salvation or be saved. The problem is His nature won't allow Him to do these things. Taking away the free will God gave to man, removes the voluntary act of choosing to do or not do something. Swooping down into a person's heart by force so they can receive salvation goes against the nature of God as well because it takes away a person's choice to accept what Christ did on the cross for themselves.

Every person has the right to accept or reject that great sacrifice Christ made – it is _their_ choice. Both scenarios defy God's nature – so He can't do these things. True love does not force, bulldoze, or bully anyone. God cannot deny His own character – not even for us. We would do well not to confuse God's ability with God's inherent nature. When we invite a revelation of His sovereign nature into the affairs of our lives, we are acknowledging His ability but permitting His essential nature to permeate our way of thinking so that our prayers are based on what He wills to be and knows is best for our lives and not our will.

> [11]*Yours, O Lord, is the greatness and the power and the glory and the victory and the majesty, indeed everything that is in the heavens and on the earth; Yours is the dominion and kingdom, O Lord, and You exalt Yourself as head over all. Both riches and honor come from You, and You rule over all. In Your hand is power and might; and it is in Your hands to make great and to give strength to everyone. 1 Chronicles 29:11-12 Amplified Bible*

CHAPTER 9

FAITHFUL & IMMUTABLE

FAITHFUL - Fidelity (dependability), steadfastness (reliability, constant), stable

IMMUTABLE - Unchanging; constant; unalterable; fixed

God's faithful and unchanging nature are the foundation of every one of His characteristics. He is indefinitely Infinite, He is perpetually Omniscient, permanently Transcendent, unalterably Righteous, and firmly Sovereign. These realities about His nature have never changed and never will. God demonstrates His faithfulness in the fulfillment of His promises and when we fully understand and accept the perfect integrity of a just and honest God, we won't hesitate to place our faith in who He is, and we won't doubt His Words to us. God's faithfulness cannot be altered and will not change. His nature does not depend on our response or lack of response. He does not sway and bend with winds of human fear and indecision.

> *If we are faithless, He remains faithful [true to His*
> *word and His righteous character], for He cannot*
> *deny himself. 2 Timothy 2:13 Amplified Bible*

We can be unfaithful when we put everything and everyone else above Him, when we devote our time and resources to feeding our fleshly desires, when we depend on our understanding above His, and when we embrace the voice of our enemy over the Words of our God. These are some of the ways that we can most assuredly be seen by the Lord as unfaithful. We're moved and influenced by all that goes on around us. Based on God's omniscient nature, anything happening, already happened because the beginning and the end are in front of Him at the same time. God's faithful and unchangeable nature defines every part of Him as trustworthy, reliable, unwavering, and dependable. Even when we ask God to change to satisfy our desires, as much as He loves us, He will not change, which is why He can't be manipulated or controlled.

When we understand His true character, our prayers will line up with the revelation of God's Will as being greater than our own. When we pray *"Your kingdom come, your will be done,"* we are really asking for the will of the Father to be present in our everyday lives; a will based on His true character, His word and His purpose for our lives.

> *6 "For I am the LORD - I do not change. That is why you are not already utterly destroyed, for My mercy endures forever. Malachi 3:6 The Living Bible*

God's faithfulness is why we can count on restoration in our lives and not utter destruction that comes from sin. Time after time when the children of Israel sinned in the Old Testament, consequences came for their rebellion, but the nature of God prevailed in offering forgiveness and restoration. The plan of God for this earth cannot be executed without Him being faithful to Himself, and faithful to His purpose concerning us. When Peter denied knowing Jesus, it would have been easy for God to allow him to be arrested or even killed, but Jesus had already ensured that Peter would play a significant role in spreading the gospel of the Kingdom and expanding the family of God. Even Peter's mistakes wouldn't ultimately be a hindrance but a tool used by a sovereign God that is able to incorporate the missteps and mistakes of His children into His foreseen purposes and cause all things to work together for the good.

Jesus' Condemnation and Peter's Denials

[54] Then they arrested Jesus, led him away, and brought him into the high priest's house. But Peter was following at a distance. [55] When they had made a fire in the middle of the courtyard and sat down together, Peter sat down among them. [56] Then a slave girl, seeing him as he sat in the firelight, stared at him and said, "This man was with him too!" [57] But Peter denied it: "Woman, I don't know him!" [58] Then a little later someone else saw him and said, "You are one of them too." But Peter said, "Man, I am not!" [59] And after about an hour still another insisted, "Certainly this man was with him, because he too is a Galilean." [60] But Peter said, "Man, I don't know what you're talking about!" At that moment, while he was still speaking, a rooster crowed.

[61] Then the Lord turned and looked straight at Peter, and Peter remembered the word of the Lord, how he had said to him, "Before a rooster crows today, you will deny me three times." [62] And he went outside and wept bitterly. Luke 22:54-62 New English Translation

Peter denied knowing Jesus and when he realized what he had done, he was filled with grief. He was overcome with guilt and shame over what he had done to the man He walked with and admired. We can only imagine what it felt like to hear that rooster crow as Jesus predicted or even more so, to have Jesus look you directly in the eyes at the precise moment of the prediction; to not discover on that third time, you had already denied him twice and didn't realize it. That's a lot to take in about yourself all at once, huh? Denying that you know someone you swore you would never deny and them finding out is rough, but denying someone who taught you, fed you and spoke life into you – that's a whole lot worse! That's why a revelation of God's faithful and unchangeable nature is so important. God had purpose for Peter just like He does for you. In a beautiful encounter by the sea you'll find Jesus restoring an embarrassed and sheepish Peter. He was able to be forgiven and restored so that purpose could be fulfilled *(John 21:15-19).* God was faithful to forgive even the one who had publicly betrayed and rejected Him.

> *⁹ If we [freely] admit that we have sinned and confess our sins, He is faithful and just [true to His own nature and promises], and will forgive our sins and cleanse us continually from all unrighteousness [our wrongdoing, everything not in conformity with His will and purpose]. 1 John 1:9 Amplified Bible*

The Lord spoke to me about His Faithful & Unchangeable nature and said:

My faithfulness and My immutability define My nature as being trustworthy reliable, dependable, and unchanging. These two characteristics give definition to all of My character, to all of My nature letting you know that I will never change and that everything about Me is trustworthy, that everything about Me is reliable, that everything about Me can be depended on. My Immutability tells you that nothing about Me is going to change and My faithfulness tells you that because I'm not going to change, that you can rely and depend on Me to remain forever just as I AM.

There will never be a time that I will come to an end; it says that you can always rely and depend on My moral purity and holiness. It will never be a time that I will have blemish or spot. You can rely and depend on Me to always exist above all My creation, always having the ability to live apart from My creation; you can trust that no one will ever be able to overpower Me or render Me powerless. You can depend on Me to be present everywhere at the same time for all time and eternity. You can rely on Me to never change in My justice, that I will always be fair.

You can trust that I will always reign supreme throughout the heavens and all the universe; that I am supreme in My very essence and that I will forever remain the Chief Ruler of the universe. There will never be a time when someone becomes qualified to take My place. Know that I will never, ever move out of My place of rule, authority, and power; that I, alone, am The Living God, from everlasting to everlasting.

My Immutability lets you know that these parts of Me will never change, that these parts of Me will remain the same, that they will always be. My Immutability lets you know that I will never deny My nature and the essence of Who I AM, not even for man's sake; for according to My Word it is impossible for Me to lie or deny My character.

Inviting the Faithful and Immutable Nature of God

One of the most important things we can do in our time with God is to focus on His nature. I saw this part of God's nature in a way that I had not seen it before when I lost my job a couple of years ago. In fact, the Lord spoke quite clearly and brought great assurance to me regarding my future from that day forward and specifically referenced His faithful and unchangeable nature. He reminded me that these parts of Him would manifest in His provision for me and He emphasized my need to hold fast to His faithful and unchangeable nature, and not to the provision I was looking for. He was showing me that my faith had to be in who He is and not what He gives me because these two characteristics define every part of who He is. So please consider all His attributes because they all contribute to an understanding of who God truly is.

At the foundation of God's character is His _faithfulness and unchangeableness_. Whenever you feel like everyone has left you or the help you depended on is suddenly unavailable, remember the truth. God remains faithful to Himself – to His nature and that makes Him faithful to everything He has spoken. We can bring the faithfulness of God into the drought seasons of our lives, when finances are depleted, options seem non-existent, and a deadline is staring us in the face. Remember who God is and the revelation you received and thank Him for being undeniably faithful to His character. Thank Him for the provision He made when He promised not to forsake or desert you. Our day to day lives need every part of God's nature to fill it. Marriages, Jobs, Parenting, School, Ministry, etc. As you invite the perfect nature of God into your day to day life, while you're in the car, in the shower, at home alone in the kitchen cooking, remember God will never respond differently from who He truly is and that every aspect of your life is more important to Him than you will ever know.

CHAPTER 10

GOD AND SATAN: TRUTH VS. LIES

¹ The serpent was the shrewdest of all the wild animals the Lord God had made. One day he asked the woman, "Did God really say you must not eat the fruit from any of the trees in the garden?" ² "Of course we may eat fruit from the trees in the garden," the woman replied. ³ "It's only the fruit from the tree in the middle of the garden that we are not allowed to eat. God said, 'You must not eat it or even touch it; if you do, you will die.'" ⁴ "You won't die!" the serpent replied to the woman. ⁵ "God knows that your eyes will be opened as soon as you eat it, and you will be like God, knowing both good and evil." ⁶ The woman was convinced. She saw that the tree was beautiful and its fruit looked delicious, and she wanted the wisdom it would give her. So she took some of the fruit and ate it. Then she gave some to her husband, who was with her, and he ate it, too. ⁷ At that moment their eyes were opened, and they suddenly felt shame at their nakedness. So they sewed fig leaves together to cover themselves. ⁸ When the cool evening breezes were blowing, the man and his

wife heard the LORD God walking about in the garden. So they hid from the LORD God among the trees. ⁹ Then the LORD God called to the man, "Where are you?" ¹⁰ He replied, "I heard you walking in the garden, so I hid. I was afraid because I was naked."

Genesis 3:1-10 New Living Translation

The devil has implied many things about the character of God since the beginning in the garden, therefore he is still doing so today by planting doubts about who God is. His question to Eve was quite clever because asking her "Did God really say?" is suggestive that God could potentially be unreliable or that He could possibly be holding out on her. If I can't trust what God says, then I will inevitably question His character without realizing that's what I'm doing. To question one's character is to place doubt on their credibility, morality, values, and their authenticity. I'm basically questioning if whether you're the real deal. Once we've placed doubt on a person's character, it's pretty impossible to trust anything they say or do. The devil knew the legitimacy of God's ability and character, but he also saw an opportunity to continue in his rebellious ways. Who better to suggest or plant a seed of doubt than with the one He made in His image, the one He gave the earth to rule and have dominion, the one He cherished: mankind.

As you can see in the passage above, it didn't take long for the serpent to slither his way into getting man to doubt God thus making them vulnerable to deception. It made it easy to accept the lie, "You won't die!" because at this point doubt had already been planted in their minds about God. The truth is what they knew and lived with everyday with God. One suggestion or idea presenting doubt changed everything for man that day. We talk a lot about the devil deceiving Eve, but the deception was made easy through the doubt that was planted. You can't really be deceived unless you've been brought to a place of doubt or uncertainty first. Our enemy, the devil, has been successful at these tactics and brought many to the place of casting blame and fault on God for everything that doesn't go our way. Many of us are listening to these ongoing recordings in our mind: "How could God let this happen? I've been a good person", "why won't God answer my prayer, he's just a child, why are you doing this to him?", "I prayed for days that God would heal my mom, but He never did, she died while I was en route to see her", "why didn't God stop him from hurting me?", "does God care at all about what's going on in the world, He's not doing anything". Any of these sound familiar? All of these questions and statements come from a place of doubt, ignorance, assumption, and misinformation. All of them question God's character.

This is the goal of our enemy the devil, to get us to question who God is thus questioning what God says. If this becomes the case, we will only withdraw from God and any notion of getting to know Him. Not getting to know God prevents us from knowing who we really are and why we are here. Here's some good news: God made man for Himself therefore He made us with a desire to know Him and need Him and that's the void within us that we spend a lifetime trying to fill that can never be filled until we meet God and get to know Him.

The devil is clever at planting counterfeit suggestions and ideas in our thoughts to make something seem more real than it is or look like something it isn't. Instead of coming right out and telling us God is not real or God is not listening, he gets us to say it as we begin to gradually doubt what we believe or know about God. Now we're bringing charges against God for what we think He should've done and didn't, for prayers we think He should've answered and wouldn't. The devil made one statement to Eve and the Bible says in Genesis 3:6, *The woman was convinced. She saw that the tree was beautiful, and its fruit looked delicious, and she wanted the wisdom it would give her.* In other words, once she doubted God's ability to take care of her, she assumed her independence and went after what might taste good, what looked appealing and satisfying and what might make her resourceful and able to take care of herself.

The devil is the one that convinces us that a shadow of death is actual death, or that his roaring and prowling around like a lion, means that he's an actual lion, to get us to deny or question in one way or another whether God is who He says He is and to make us doubt the truth. For the believer, death is only a shadow and the devil can only seek to devour us. These have all been shrewd efforts manufactured by the devil to get us to continue on with what Adam and Eve did – live independently of God and pursue provision and purpose on our own. These efforts interfere with the gospel of the Kingdom impacting and enveloping the entire earth. Its shrewd, but not final!

This is why it is particularly important to have the right view of God, based on the real truth. Discovery of His nature is ALL about learning and experiencing who He "truly" is, and the rights and privileges that we have received from God as his heirs, possessing the Spirit of God for the purpose of establishing His Kingdom on the earth like it is in heaven.

Our view and perception of God determines whether we walk at a distance from a God that is our Father, or if we walk in the cool of a day with our Father who just happens to be God Almighty. Life circumstances, traumatic experiences and mishandling by people have trained us to believe the lies trafficked in by our enemy.

One of the devil's chief weapons is the same one he used with Eve: Doubt. It is still one of his best weapons today, to successfully get us to doubt who God is and to "convince" us like he did Eve that God will let us down, that we need to "handle our business" ourselves, do what we have to do to protect ourselves since it "sounds" like God might leave us hanging. Since then our Father has wanted only for us to see and know the truth.

Knowing the nature of God can expose the lies we tend to embrace when difficult situations arise, and our belief systems are flawed with assumptions, expectations and values from our ancestors and influential circles. Perceptions are born out of situations and experiences and become so vivid and real to us that we embrace it as the irrefutable truth. But these things that we have resolved as truth, have not brought us understanding, freedom, peace, or joy – just more questions, frustration and even bitterness.

Because a road that doesn't have truth will only lead to a dead end. We have learned at this point, that revelation from God is what's True. Everything God is and all He says is Truth. The Bible tells us in John 8:44 that Satan, the devil, does not stand in the truth because there is no truth in him. That when he lies, he speaks what's natural to him because he is a liar. So, when we gain an understanding of the nature of God, we are coming into the fullness of what truth really is.

> *46 I have come as Light into the world, so that everyone who believes and trusts in Me [as Savior-all those who anchor their hope in Me and rely on the truth of My message] will not continue to live in darkness. John 12:46 Amplified Bible*

The lies we have believed about God's character have hindered our growth and kept us from personally experiencing His wonderful attributes. The lies that bring darkness can be overcome when we allow the light of God's truth to be revealed from the Spirit of God. The devil's issue isn't really with man, it's with God due to the devil's pride that's as big as the universe. The thought of having all power and control is intoxicating and alluring – enough to cause one to rebel against the Highest Sovereign in a futile attempt to gain it.

Manipulating and influencing us to rebel against our Source and His authenticity is a strategic power play to overthrow our inherited position of power and relationship. When we buy into the lie that He loves us based on what we do, or how well we serve, or how much money we can give, we are missing the truth about the nature of God. When we accuse Him of ignoring us or refusing to answer us or it is taking too long, we miss the opportunity to build a faith that comes from trusting in who God is, not what He gives us. If I trust that He is dependable and trustworthy and knows who I am and what's happening in my life, I can trust that His silence is not about hurting me or betraying me. Personally, some of my best training has been in the silent times with God; training me to trust, to think differently about Him, and to rely on Him without wavering.

I am committed to live in submission to faith in God's character. I spent enough years relying *only* on what He said and didn't know what to do with myself when He wasn't saying something or if years and years went by and nothing happened. There was no peace in that, only stress and frustration that made me the princess of pouting. Trusting in who He is makes the difference because even if God doesn't intervene or situations don't change, my faith is in what never changes: His character. Having faith in His character empowered me to trust God when I wasn't hearing or seeing anything different in the things going on around me. When you know His nature in a personal way, the lies and doubts in your life will be exposed as such, because God will never respond differently from who He truly is. No matter how much we mess up, accuse God, shut down, pout, or even walk away, He will never stop being the righteous, holy God who loves us with a perfect Love. A Love that would never ignore or torment, or keep a record of all the pouting, accusations, and walk-outs.

The Truth of God is everything He is and all that He's ready to reveal to us. The lie is that we should trust God only if He comes through for what we want, and that God can't be fully known because He is too distant, too mysterious, and too inconsistent. If you want to know the truth about God, be willing to engage Him personally with a pure motive; not for self-serving, self-entitled reasons or what you can gain.

I would encourage you to put your belief systems and convictions up against what God begins to reveal as you explore and learn more about His character and yours. If what we hold to be true is really true, it will align with the Truth that's revealed to us by the Lord. Anything that you've held to be true that hasn't produced the peace of God will most likely be tested by what God begins to reveal. You will find that some things will blow your mind and challenge what you've learned from your ancestors and people of influence in your life. Real truth is revealed when we willingly engage God because we want to get to know God, for who He truly is. Real truth that is revealed by God makes you free. <>

CPSIA information can be obtained
at www.ICGtesting.com
Printed in the USA
BVHW031438041020
590263BV00001B/3

9 781728 360560